COULD THE MILITARY GOVERN THE PHILIPPINES?

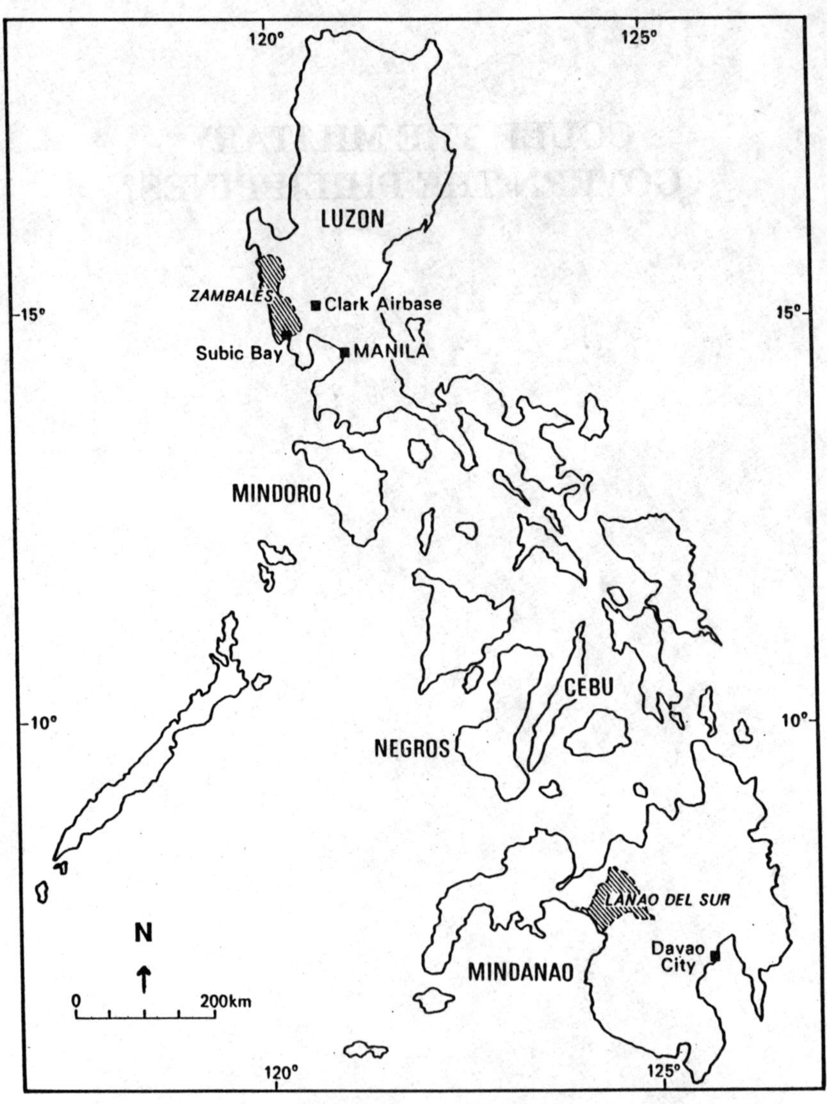

The Philippines, showing major places named in the text

COULD THE MILITARY GOVERN THE PHILIPPINES?

Viberto Selochan

New Day Publishers
Quezon City, Philippines
1989

Published by
New Day Publishers
11 Lands St., Project 6
P.O. Box 167, 1100 Quezon City
Philippines

The views presented in this publication
do not necessarily reflect that of New Day Publishers.
The author is responsible for his own analysis
and conclusions.

Cover Design: Toti Orias

ISBN 971-10-0399-6

Contents

Frontispiece, The Map of the Philippines   ii

Foreword   vii

Preface   ix

Abbreviations   xi

1   INTRODUCTION   1

2   ROLE IN NATIONAL DEVELOPMENT   3

3   PROPOSED RIGHTS TO GOVERN   8

4   MANAGING OPPOSITION   16
     A. The Communist Party,   16
     B. The Muslim Insurgents,   19
     C. Business and Politicians,   20
     D. The Church,   26
     E. The Perceived Reactions from the Population,   28

5   INTERNATIONAL RESPONSE   29
      A. US Recognition,   29
      B. ASEAN and Other Asian Nations,   32

6   FUTURE PROSPECTS   35

7   CONCLUSION   41

Appendices
      Appendix 1 AFP Command Structure,   45
      Appendix 2 AFP Strength and Firepower,   46

References   49

Foreword

Viberto Selochan paints a fascinating, yet disturbing, portrait of the military in the Philippine political process. His book is a contribution to the comparative literature on civilian control of the military in the Third World, as well as to the analysis of political change in the Philippines. Much of its interest derives from the fact that it is based on interviews with members and ex-members of the Armed Forces of the Philippines (AFP) themselves.

The Philippines has faced—indeed still faces—economic, political and "security" contradictions every bit as serious as those that have precipitated coups in other developing countries. Why, then, has the military not intervened? Mr. Selochan attempts to answer this question. But in so doing, he demonstrates convincingly that the question itself may be somewhat misleading. For although the AFP have never governed in their own right, they have been a "major" player in the political game all through the post World War II period. Moreover they have been sustained in this role through their close links with the United States. Although US military assistance may have contributed to their professionalization, the latter has been of a uniquely political kind. Except during the unique circumstances surrounding the overthrow of the Marcos regime, the military has maintained a veto on progressive politics, as well as on the termination or modification of US military base rights in the country.

Mr. Selochan describes the coup attempts against the present government of Mrs. Corazon Aquino, and concludes that future attempts could well be more successful if the economic situation continues to deteriorate. A number of the military men and business leaders he talked to apparently subscribe to the view that some form of military or "strong" government might be required to put the Philippines back on the path of development. However, he is rightly skeptical about the prospects for these authoritarian "fixes" for the country's manifold difficulties. Although "bureaucratic-authoritarian" or "repressive- developmental" regimes have promoted economic growth in countries such as Brazil, Korea or Indonesia, the circumstances have been unique in each case. And there are just as many examples of such regimes that have failed to bring prosperity, as in Chile, Argentina, Bangladesh, Ethiopia or Nigeria. The Philippines' military establishment is probably too closely linked to vested interests, and too divided internally, to act as a genuine motor of transformation. This book provides a useful overview both of its potential and of its limitations.

A. Robin Luckham
Visiting Fellow
   Peace Research Centre
   Research School of Pacific Studies
   The Australian National University
   Canberra, Australia, and
Senior Fellow
   Institute of Development Studies
   University of Sussex
   Sussex, England

Canberra, Australia
July 12, 1989

Preface

The Armed Forces of the Philippines (AFP) were pivotal in maintaining Pres. Ferdinand Marcos in office, just as they were in his demise and the accession of Mrs. Corazon Aquino to the presidency. Because of their role in the latter, it appears that elements in the officer corps expected Pres. Corazon Aquino to reward them with positions commensurable with their contribution to her achieving the presidency. But democracy returned to the Philippines, and it required that the AFP remain subservient to the civilian commander-in-chief and protect the citizens from internal violence and external attack.

Officers unprepared to accept these requirements were ready to destabilize the Aquino administration and achieve their goals through attempted coups. Other officers were, however, prepared to protect the newly regained democracy which they swear to uphold.

It was between these two groups that I was caught during my research in the Philippines, and spent hours debating the merits and demerits of the democratic system versus the authoritarian system. Many expected that because of my work on the Latin American armed forces that I would have an abhorrence of government by the military and staunchly support democracy. Meanwhile, other officers tried to argue that military rule is a means of solving the problems of the Philippines, as military governments had achieved "successes" in countries such as South Korea. To neither view did I openly subscribe, since I was there to ascertain the views of the officers. These views prompted me to write this paper to make known to the Philippine society a debate that is presently taking place which if not resolved could have ramifications for Philippine domestic and international politics.

Without the assistance of officers of the AFP who gave so generously of their time, both while on duty and in their leisure time, I would not have been able to write this book. Therefore it is to them I dedicate it. Despite the image that is portrayed at times, there are many officers who are committed to making the AFP a truly Filipino institution for the protection of Filipinos.

Special thanks are also due to Secretary of Defense Fidel Ramos, who as AFP chief of staff gave me permission to undertake this study; and to Col. Oscar Florendo and the staff of the Public Information Office at Camp Aguinaldo, especially Mrs. Grace Matutina, who were always willing to provide me with permission to travel and interview officers throughout the Philippine islands. To the officers who acted as liaison while I was in the different services, especially PC Maj. Rodolfo Roderos and Army Capt. Ricardo Morales, I express my sincere gratitude. Finally, to the many other Filipinos who generously assisted me while I was undertaking this research, my thanks.

Viberto Selochan

August 1989

Abbreviations

ADAM	National Alliance for Democracy and Morality
AFP	Armed Forces of the Philippines
ANP	Alliance for New Politics
ASEAN	Association of South East Asian Nations
BAC-UP	Bacolod Citizens for Unity and Peace
BAYAN	Bagong Alyansang Makabayan (New Patriotic Alliance)
BMILO	Bangsa Minsupala Islamic Liberation Organization
BMLO	Bangsa Moro Liberation Organization
CA	Commission on Appointments
CARP	Comprehensive Agrarian Reform Program
CHDF	Civilian Home Defense Forces
CMO	Civil Military Operations
CPP	Communist Party of the Philippines
EDSA	Epifanio de los Santos Avenue, Metro Manila

GAD	Grand Alliance for Democracy
Huks	Hukbalahap (Hukbo ng Bayan Laban sa Hapon)
INP	Integrated National Police
JUSMAG	Joint United States Military Advisory Group
KBL	Kilusang Bagong Lipunan (New Society Movement)
MILF	Moro Islamic Liberation Front
MNLF	Moro National Liberation Front
MNLF-RG	Moro National Liberation Front Reformist Group
NDF	National Democratic Front
NMFD	National Movement for Freedom and Democracy
NP	Nacionalista Party
NPA	New People's Army
PC	Philippine Constabulary
PCFC	Philippine Constabulary Forward Command
PMA	Philippine Military Academy
PnB	Partido ng Bayan (People's Party)
RAM	Reform the Armed Forces Movement
ROTC	Reserve Officer Training Corps
SEATO	South East Asia Treaty Organization
SOTs	Special Operations Teams
UNIDO	United Nationalist Democratic Organization
Unladbayan	National Movement for Economic Reconstruction and Survival or Nation Movers
VPD	Volunteers for Popular Democracy

1

INTRODUCTION

The Armed Forces of the Philippines (AFP) played a central role in President Marcos' imposition of martial law in September 1972. The military was then instrumental in maintaining Marcos in power and in the process became a partner in government. Fourteen years later the military participated in the events of February 1986 that drove Marcos into abandoning the presidency, thus allowing Mrs. Corazon Aquino to assume that office.

However, dissensions between the Aquino administration and certain groups in the armed forces developed shortly and these have culminated in seven coup attempts. Of these, the one led by Col. Gregorio "Gringo" Honasan on 28 August 1987 came dangerously close to achieving its objectives. Colonel Honasan was captured and placed in custody for his role in the coup. But a few months later he escaped and continues to evade his captors. On 12 April 1988, ten days after his escape, Brig. Gen. Rodolfo Biazon, the National Capital Region District Commander (Manila), who was in charge of the operation to recapture Honasan, claimed that the colonel had planned with retired and active duty officers for the establishment of a junta which could govern the Philippines at some unspecified date (*Philippine Daily Globe*, 12 April 1988). To achieve this objective, the group will need the support of a large section of the AFP, especially the army. If it succeeds in seizing power, it raises an important question: could the military govern the Philippines?

In this paper I will attempt to demonstrate that various administrations in the Philippines have assisted officers in the armed forces to acquire the skills of government and fanned the desire to govern by appointing retired and active duty officers to positions in government. In turn, some of these officers have acquired the perception that the military can govern and have staged several unsuccessful coups to put their theory to the test. The 1987 Constitution prohibits the Aquino administration from appointing active duty officers to positions in government, but retired officers continue to be placed in these positions. Because of these appointments, many active duty officers are encouraged to believe that the AFP should play a significant role in the politics of the nation.

2

ROLE IN NATIONAL DEVELOPMENT

The Philippines was administered by colonial military governors during the Spanish and early period of American tutelage. After achieving independence from the United States in 1946, the islands were described as the "showcase of democracy" in Asia. Such a description was based on the premise that the essentially American principles of Western democracy had become firmly entrenched in the Philippines. Yet soon after the Philippines became independent, the communist-influenced HUKBALAHAP (*Hukbo ng Bayan Laban sa Hapon*) or Resistance to the Japanese Occupation in Central Luzon better known as "Huks" threatened this supposition. The Huks became rebels when both American and Filipino officials refused to recognize their contribution in the war against the Japanese. Open hostilities ensued between the AFP and the Huks who were at one stage perceived to be a danger to the seat of government in Manila.

The extensive campaign to defeat the Huks was conducted by the armed forces. It was, however, not confined to armed combat; since it was also a peasant movement fighting for agrarian reforms. Rather, under the direction of Secretary of Defense Ramon Magsaysay, the strategy became a combination of political, socioeconomic and military activities. The Huks were claimed to have been defeated first politically then militarily (Bello, 1987:9-25). Arguably so, but the campaign was conducted predominantly by the Philippine military under a civilian politician and with the assistance of the Joint U.S. Military Advisory Group (JUSMAG), through US Col. Edward Lansdale and his assistant US Army Capt. Charles Bohannan.

Secretary Ramon Magsaysay had been a guerrilla officer during the Second World War. After liberation, the US Army appointed him military governor of the province of Zambales before he entered Congress. Magsaysay became the first Defense secretary in the Philippines to be given complete control over the armed forces as a result of American pressure on Pres. Elpidio Quirino. As secretary of Defense, Magsaysay worked closely with the military, with support from his US military adviser, Colonel Lansdale. It is alleged that Lansdale and his assistant were primarily responsible for Magsaysay's perceptions of the military and of its role as a force in national development because of its performance during the Huk campaign.

Ramon Magsaysay was elected president of the Philippines in 1953 with the support of the US government. And indeed the Philippine military identified Magsaysay as the presidential champion of its institutional objectives (Goldberg, 1976:108). Modelling his government on that of Kemal Ataturk's of Turkey, President Magsaysay appointed officers to positions in government. Like Ataturk, Magsaysay wanted the officers to resign their commissions before accepting government appointments. Among the officers appointed were Col. Fred Ruiz Castro, as Magsaysay's executive secretary, and Maj. Jose Crisol, as acting director of the National Bureau of Investigation (NBI) and then undersecretary of National Defense.

In accordance with his avowed policy of strengthening security, Magsaysay appointed a large number of officers to the Department of Defense. Col. Sotero Cabahug became secretary of Defense, Col. Nicanor Jimenez headed the department's Public Affairs Office, while Capt. Rodolfo Andal was in charge of the finance section. A number of junior officers were also employed in the department. In other sectors of government, Brig. Gen. Eleuterio Adevoso was appointed secretary of Labor, Maj. Mariano Yengco was promoted to assistant minister of Executive Office, Lt. Col. Jaime Ferrer became undersecretary of Agriculture and National Resources, Lt. Col. Frisco San Juan, chairman of the Presidential Complaints Action Committee, Col. Salvador Villa, general manager of Manila Railroad Company, Col. Jaime Velasquez, commissioner of Customs, Col. Osmundo Mondoñedo, chief of the Agricultural Credit and Cooperative Financing Administration and

Capt. Ernesto Jimenez, general manager of the Central Cooperative Exchange. Other government sectors headed by active duty officers were the Home Financing Administration, the National Resettlement and Rehabilitation Administration, the National Rice and Corn Corporation and Government Service Insurance System. Malacañang, the presidential palace, was predominantly staffed by officers. Capt. Edgardo Tolentino became chief of the Palace Records Department and Capt. Rodolfo Andal, finance officer. Among his personal staff were Capt. Noli Reyes, the president's private secretary and Col. Mamerto Montemayor his legal adviser. President Magsaysay also relied on a coterie of retired and active duty officers for advice. As a result, the armed forces developed strong links with the government.

Magsaysay's death in an air crash in 1957 threatened to terminate these links. Officers close to the president knew that Carlos Garcia was only acceptable as vice president to Magsaysay because he posed no threat to Magsaysay's campaign for re-election. Garcia was isolated from the president's "inner circle" and was not generally involved in decision-making. Therefore, the military perceived him as being inadequately prepared for the presidency. Vice President Garcia was attending a meeting of the South East Asian Treaty Organization (SEATO) in Australia when President Magsaysay was killed. Certain elements in the military wanted to capitalize on this perceived opportunity to govern by seizing power and appointing former AFP Chief of Staff Gen. Jesus Vargas, as president. With little confidence in Garcia's ability to govern, the incentive to seize power was compelling. Amidst the uncertainties surrounding Magsaysay's death, however, the military was unable to consolidate its power quickly. In the meantime Carlos Garcia returned to assume the mantle of office as mandated by the Philippine Constitution.

Unlike Magsaysay, the next two presidents of the Philippines, Carlos Garcia and Diosdado Macapagal, were not overtly supported in their presidential elections by the US nor the military. Therefore, as president, they appointed politicians to positions in government thus displacing many military officers appointed to civilian positions by Magsaysay. Nevertheless, elements in the AFP officer corps still believed that the AFP should play a major role in national politics. In 1958, after only one year of Garcia's presidency, there were plans for a coup to replace the president with Defense Secretary Jesus Vargas (Constantino, 1984:305-306). After dismissing the Defense secretary, Garcia spent the rest of his presidency trying unsuccessfully to legislate against active duty officers being appointed to ministerial positions. On the other hand, officers determined to regain political power formed the Grand Alliance Party in July 1959 to compete against the incumbent in the presidential elections of that year. Garcia's experiences with the military contributed to his successor's (Macapagal) distrust of the AFP. Macapagal tried to curb its power by rotating AFP chiefs of staff and the Philippine Constabulary (PC) chiefs. In his four-year term as president, Macapagal established a record for having eight chiefs of staff and four PC chiefs.

In 1965 President Macapagal's successor to the office was Ferdinand Marcos. Like Magsaysay, Marcos was a guerrilla officer and claimed to have been the most decorated soldier in the Philippines for his role in the Second World War (Crisol & Baclagon, 1983) a claim that has been refuted (McDougald, 1987:5-97). Marcos nevertheless used his military background to strengthen his relationship with the armed forces. To further enhance those relations, President Marcos maintained the Defense portfolio during the first thirteen months of his presidency, and was directly responsible for the promotion of many officers, thus establishing a patronage system in promotions. It has been argued that Marcos courted the military because early in his political career he had decided to use martial law as a pretext for "perpetuating himself in power" (Brillantes, 1987:86).

Martial law, declared on 21 September 1972, presented a new challenge to the military. Relegated to reorganization and training during the two previous administrations, the armed forces once again felt "*malakas* [strong] with Malacañang" (Goldberg, 1976:109). Officers were appointed to administer a range of government departments and private corporations. Most of these corporations had been sequestered from Marcos opponents and included those of his vice president, Fernando Lopez, and those of the Elizalde and Jacinto families. The latter were placed under the chairmanship of the AFP chief of staff, Gen. Romeo Espino. As a result, the military assumed a high profile in political and economic life in the Philippines following a pattern that had already been established in Indonesia also as a result of martial law. Now not only was the AFP performing military duties, but officers were also in positions traditionally occupied by politicians. In the process, the military not only dispensed justice but also political patronage, formerly the exclusive domain of politicians (Hernandez, 1985:1085).

Despite its active participation in government under Magsaysay, the AFP generally played a limited role in national politics until becoming

6

a partner in government with Marcos. What lessons have these experiences provided to the officer corps? According to retired and active duty officers, civilian politicians have relied on the military when governing. Therefore, civilians have never had the monopoly on administering the Philippines. From its experiences some elements in the military perceive that it could participate directly in national development and that it can successfully govern the Philippines, like the armed forces in a number of other Asian countries such as Indonesia, Thailand and South Korea.

The results of a survey among 500 officers conducted in April-May 1987 serves to substantiate these claims (Miranda & Ciron, 1987). Of the officers responding to the questionnaires, 96 per cent claimed that the military had an important role to play in national development, which was defined as "an economically and politically secure environment." And 43 per cent stated that the military should temporarily take over the government to prevent the communists from doing so. Indeed it can be argued that when the level of politicization of the officer corps is high so is the possibility for military intervention in politics. But what would be the reasons the armed forces could offer to justify the claim of being capable of governing?

3

PROFESSED RIGHTS TO GOVERN

Probably the most cogent reason presently used by some military men to justify its right to govern is the role it played in the events between 22-25 February 1986 on Epifanio de los Santos Avenue (EDSA), Quezon City, that led to the downfall of Marcos. The opportunity then existed for the military to seize power. According to many officers, it had the power to "take-over the country" and plans had indeed been drawn up for the armed forces to replace Marcos. Instead, the AFP gave power to the civilians. Consequently, the military appears to be claiming the right to determine who governs and when. Retired Brig. Gen. Eduardo M. Garcia (1988), commenting on the situation in the Philippines, observed that:

All professions and occupations have their rightful places and uses in our society. The politicians have theirs. And so with the men in uniform, and the military and police. At certain times, however, the politicians can be dispensed with, as during the one year and four months of the Aquino revolutionary government. But the military can never be dispensed with.

This typical military perception sees the AFP as having been instrumental in maintaining stability in the society during Aquino's incumbency. Furthermore, politicians are viewed as non-essentials.

Could it be that the military is again of the opinion that the time is right to dispense with the politicians, and to reclaim the power it allegedly gave to them?

HIGH EDUCATIONAL REQUIREMENTS

The AFP prides itself on having a highly educated officer corps. To become an officer it is necessary to have a bachelor's degree. Graduates from the Philippine Military Academy (PMA) obtain a Bachelor of Science degree after four years, and this entitles them to become regular officers. Presently they comprise 22 per cent of the officer corps. The remaining officers are predominantly reservists who have a degree from a Philippine college acquired after completing the educational curriculum and the military requirements of the Reserve Officers Training Course (ROTC). Apart from military courses undertaken by officers as part of the educational and career requirements, many officers claim that they undertake additional studies in civilian educational institutions. These courses are mostly in management, business administration, political science and economics, and are generally undertaken at educational establishments such as the prestigious Asian Institute of Management in Makati, Manila. A small percentage undertake a similar curriculum in overseas institutions, mainly in the US and increasingly Australia. By undertaking courses in the social sciences, officers learn that security is not solely confined to military power. They also discover that security depends on political, social and economic policies. Although further education enhances professionalism, it can also endanger a civilian government that is perceived to be performing inadequately by the officers, since their education may serve to promote critical evaluation of existing political institutions and their incumbents.

Because the majority of officers allegedly undertake advanced degree courses, there is a perception in the AFP that the officer corps is highly educated. Yet according to statistics obtained from the general headquarters of the AFP, only 4 per cent of the 16,000-strong officer corps have higher degrees. The reasons are that the majority of officers are stationed in the provinces where access to educational institutions is limited. These officers are not encouraged or motivated to pursue further education. Most are unwilling to return to Manila to undertake such courses as this would mean having to leave their families and incurring extra financial burdens as no official assistance is provided.

In addition, leaving the provinces temporarily to undertake studies in Manila entails the loss of provincial allowances. Yet President Marcos used the pretext of a highly educated officer corps to justify his practice of appointing AFP officers to positions in government, private corporations, and as mayors, provincial governors and ambassadors.

When Mrs. Aquino became president, she espoused a policy of reconciliation. The military interpreted this to mean that officers who worked with the previous regime or who did not immediately support the breakaway group from the AFP at the February 1986 "revolution" at EDSA would not be disadvantaged. But on assuming office the government removed these officers from civilian and military positions and sent them to perform combat duties in areas where the insurgency situation is critical. Removing officers associated with the previous regime from positions in Manila may have been necessary for the esteem and preservation of the new administration. But what appears to have been expected of these officers was for them to immediately change their commitment and loyalty from the Marcos regime to the Aquino administration. During normal transfer of political office, such as the transition of power after elections, this process is gradual. Yet in a period of rapid political change it is expected to be accomplished more quickly. Meanwhile, officers associated with the events at EDSA were promoted and given "comfortable positions" in Manila, following recommendations from Gen. Fidel V. Ramos, then AFP chief of staff. Examples are: chiefs of the services and divisions and the key members of the Reform the Armed Forces of the Philippines Movement (RAM). Presently there is a group of retired and active duty officers who had served in government, but are now disenfranchised. Many of these officers concede that they "are waiting to be called to serve the country again."

Factionalism continues to exist in the AFP in spite of General Ramos' decree to disband all factions in March 1987. For a group in the AFP planning to seize power these factions could present problems, especially as some officers loyal to the government will inevitably oppose military takeover. In Latin America, when factionalism appeared to hinder military intervention in politics, the opposing officers were removed in bloody and bloodless purges. Examples are: Guatemala and Venezuela in 1962, Argentina in 1963, the Dominican Republic in 1965 and Bolivia in 1970 and 1971 (Nordlinger, 1977:44). There is no doubt that such a situation could occur in the Philippines.

Deprived of their professed rights to govern, elements in the AFP resorted to the traditional method employed by many Third World armed forces to attain this objective: coups. In the Philippines, such machinations are a new phenomenon (Muego, 1987:151; Nemenzo, 1987:9).

Between July 1986 and August 1987, seven coup attempts were staged against the Aquino administration by elements in the armed forces. Yet all were not expected to succeed, and none was successful. The purpose was to test the government's ability to withstand destabilization and to measure its "people power" support, and also to reassert the influence elements in the AFP felt it had lost since the demise of the Marcos regime. Clearly, there were lessons to be learnt by the Aquino administration in its policies towards the armed forces. A brief examination of the most significant of the attempted coups will reveal some of the major issues.

The first attempted coup played out at the Manila Hotel on 6 July 1986 was a caricature of a comic opera. It was staged by three Marcos loyalist generals and approximately 300 soldiers who were "members of the Guardians Brotherhood, Inc., a military mutual-aid society" with Lt. Col. Gregorio Honasan as its president (McCoy, 1987:25; Nemenzo, 1987:14; 1988:262-263). The intention was for Arturo Tolentino, the vice presidential running-mate of former president Marcos in the 1986 presidential elections, to occupy the office of president of the Philippines until Marcos returned. Trying to link this coup attempt with RAM, which was formed by members of the Philippine Military Academy (PMA) class of 1971 to restore professionalism to the military, elements of the Ramos faction in the military declared that Lt. Col. Gregorio Honasan was a leader of the Guardians. But, according to a number of the Guardian leaders and some members of the RAM core group, Honasan indeed wanted to control the Guardians and bring it under the umbrella of the RAM, but was unable to achieve this because of major differences between the two fraternities. Importantly, the members of the RAM were predominantly PMA graduates and the Guardians were mostly reservist officers and enlisted men. Moreover, the RAM developed because of the preference reservists received in comparison to the regular officers during Gen. Fabian Ver's tenure as the AFP chief of staff. Similarly, the attempted coup was linked to the Defense secretary of the Aquino and also the Marcos administration, Juan Ponce

Enrile (McCoy, 1987:25). Yet Enrile retained his post in the administration, while the punishment for soldiers involved in this incident was minimal and was certain to present future problems for the AFP.

Determined to destabilize the Aquino government, Enrile and the RAM made public statements questioning the legitimacy of the administration. Prepared to undermine it, the core group of the movement planned the "God Save the Queen" coup to be executed in November 1986 when President Aquino was on an official visit to Japan. For this purpose Navy Capt. Rex Robles informed Victor Corpus, whom he had recruited to work with his "Study Group" at the Ministry of Defense, to devise a new strategy for the AFP's insurgency campaign. This was prior to the reinstatement of Corpus in the AFP in November 1986 with the rank of lieutenant colonel, when a letter regarding his defection from the NPA would be used to destabilize the government and could "further enhance the scenario for a coup" (Corpus, 1987:ix). Corpus, however, disclosed the plans of the attempted coup to the chief of staff, allegedly, because he was "rabidly loyal to Ramos and the President" (Nemenzo, 1987:15; 1988:264). To abort the coup, the AFP Chief of Staff Gen. Fidel Ramos, removed the conspirators from the Ministry of Defense where they were working, and stationed them in regional commands.

Intensifying the destabilizing strategies, another coup was planned by the RAM for 22 November 1986 to replace the Aquino administration with a civilian-military regime. Simultaneous uprisings by soldiers in all military camps were to coincide with the convening of a session by members of the former Marcos Batasang Pambansa (National Assembly). But again, the AFP chief of staff aborted the attempt, despite efforts to elicit his support for the coup by, among others, Vice President Salvador Laurel (McCoy, 1987:28). Defense Secretary Juan Ponce Enrile was finally dismissed two days later for his alleged involvement in this coup attempt.

After failing to execute its coup plans on two occasions, the RAM core group decided to retreat and reassess its strategies. Members were again urged to re-read Luttak's (1968) *Coup D'Etat: A Practical Handbook*. And apparently they did. Incidentally, the RAM members had already read, *The Thai Young Turks* (1982), an account of the April 1981 attempted coup in Thailand, in order to avoid making the same mistakes committed by the Thai officers in their quest for power.

Not directly responsible for, but providing support, the RAM was again linked to another attempted coup on 27 January 1987 which was led by Gen. Jose Maria Zumel, who commanded some members of the Guardians. Executed a few days before the 2 February plebiscite to endorse the new Constitution, it was intended to reinstate former president Marcos in office. But when the US prevented Marcos from leaving Hawaii, and General Ramos ordered the arrest of a number of pro-Marcos generals, the coup fizzled out, compounded with the overwhelming support for the new Constitution. The RAM was instrumental in dissuading General Ramos from using force against the soldiers under Col. Oscar Canlas who almost gained control of a television station in Manila. But some claim that General Ramos was also reluctant to give orders to the government troops to attack the rebel soldiers, because he feared his orders might not be obeyed (Nemenzo, 1988:266). Optimistically, Professor McCoy described this attempted coup as the "final" one, and further claimed that when the new Constitution was approved, "coup rumours ended and stability returned" (1987:28-29).

Less than a month later, however, and before the scheduled congressional elections, Marcos loyalist troops again staged a revolt. On 18 April 1987 a small group of soldiers released about 108 of their imprisoned comrades involved in the January 1987 attempted coup from the army's detention center, at Fort Bonifacio in Metro Manila, and in the process occupied the army headquarters. The small size of the rebel force notwithstanding, it took the military approximately nine hours to terminate what the AFP terms the "Black Saturday" incident. According to a senior army officer, this incident highlighted the lack of discipline and the disregard of the chain of command, since the breakout was instigated by enlisted personnel.

Just when the institutions of democracy were functioning, providing the opportunity for stability, the RAM staged its most concerted effort to seize political power. More carefully organized and planned than its previous efforts, and with support from regional commands, the movement intended to overthrow the Aquino government on 28 August 1987. The plan was to establish a junta and hold presidential elections when stability was ensured. But this was certainly not an option it would have pursued in a hurry. Officers generally make such statements after seizing political power, but seldom fulfill them. Succinctly put, "the military engage in politics with relative haste but disengage with the greatest reluctance" (Finer, 1975:24).

Characterized by excessive violence, unlike other attempts, the last coup attempt certainly intended to displace President Aquino. Therefore, attacking the presidential palace was not viewed as "diversionary," but seemed to exhibit the hallmark of the February 1986 coup plans (de Dios, 1988:302). Supported by approximately 2,000 officers and men, this coup attempt solicited empathy from many others in the AFP. As a result many officers did not immediately support the government. Most waited, until they were certain which side would be victorious before deciding to pledge their support. Realizing that the government forces would be successful, the fence-sitters then supported the administration, and were dubbed "the 5 o'clock movers," according to officers interviewed. Despite the severity of this attempted coup, the government did not subject these rebels to military tribunals as was anticipated. It was abundantly clear to the AFP general staff, and the Aquino administration that there was overwhelming support in the AFP to rectify the grievances expressed by the coup leaders, even at the PMA where cadets staged a strike and were prepared to support the rebel troops in Manila. Government response to the rebellion was to quickly grant pay and allowance increases. Likewise, the AFP 1988 budget was overwhelmingly approved by the Congress making it "the second biggest recipient and the only institution whose allocation Congress increased despite driving an added 4 per cent in government deficits" (de Dios, 1988:314). Commenting on the coup attempt, military personnel claim that without it they would not have acquired the promised remunerations. One influential senior officer stated, "the coup showed the president we have the guns. We brought her to her knees." Retired General Rodolfo Canieso stated, "It [the coup attempt] was intended to send a message to the politicians."

Marking the anniversary of the 28 August 1987 attempted coup, the RAM issued a poster which read, "Our dreams shall never die." Apparently the RAM still aimed to achieve "good government and a complete revamp of the AFP." To date, the leader of the coup, former lieutenant colonel Gregorio Honasan, who was later captured and then escaped, remains a fugitive despite reports that he has visited his family in Marikina. Whether the AFP hierarchy does indeed want to recapture Honasan remains moot. Considering that many of the grievances the RAM espoused still persist, resulting in continued support for the movement in the AFP, it is unlikely that the government seriously wants to recapture him and make him a cause celebre of the armed forces. Perhaps this will change once substantial reforms have been instituted in the military. The AFP hierarchy contends that since the 28 August 1987 coup attempt, the RAM has lost its support and has disbanded. While this assertion is difficult to verify, it is reported that

14

another "loose network of officers," which shares the grievances of the RAM have taken the movement's place (FEER, 24 November 1988).

As was abundantly clear the initial coups against the Aquino administration were indeed staged to test the government's stability, and indeed whether the president could rely on "People Power" for support. Of all, the 28 August 1987 coup attempt demonstrates that elements in the military and the society are reluctant to accept the right of the Aquino administration to govern. In relation to the military, the coup attempts proved that it had not reverted to pursuing the AFP's mission of combatting the insurgents, while abandoning the desire to participate in politics.

To curb the armed forces' political machinations, advisers of the Aquino administration unanimously agreed that "the military had to be disciplined and relegated to a subservient role in the new government" (de Dios, 1988:306). Concurring with this view, former president Diosdado Macapagal, in a speech at the Makati Rotary Club on 16 October 1987, declared that the military must be restrained from intervening in the formulation of government policy. But, as Ret. Gen. Florencio Magsino warned, "The AFP is no longer the pushover it was before martial law" (The Financial Post, 27 November 1987).

How a military acts politically is determined by the sociopolitical and economic events prevailing in the society and how civilian groups react and also on the internal situation in the military. A group within the AFP that perceives itself capable of governing may now realize that it will need to wait until political events warrant its intervention. These elements will inevitably have contingency plans on how they will manage internal military and civilian opposition.

4

MANAGING OPPOSITION

A. The Communist Party

Should the military govern, its most violent opposition will come from the military wing of the Communist Party of the Philippines (CPP): the New People's Army (NPA). Therefore it has contingency plans on how to deal with the insurgents. It will adopt a two- pronged approach, which will be executed simultaneously. Firstly it will move to counteract the CPP propaganda to undermine the CPP's support base, and secondly it will continue the military campaign but with increased ferocity.

According to elements of the AFP officer corps, the insurgency situation in the Philippines has exacerbated since President Aquino assumed office because of her "soft approach" to Communism. The ranks of the NPA have increased and its activities now extend to Manila. A contributory factor has been the 60-day ceasefire agreement negotiated between the government and the National Democratic Front (NDF), the umbrella organization of the Left. Despite requests by its senior personnel, the AFP was not a party to the negotiations until military issues were discussed. Therefore, government negotiators could not profess to speak for the AFP. Thus, it was not surprising that the military expressed antipathy towards the agreement. The CPP claim that the Aquino government negotiated a ceasefire because of the inefficiency and demoralized state of the AFP and the president's desire to consolidate her power over it. But according to senior officers at the AFP General Headquarters in Camp Aguinaldo, the ceasefire was intended to give the armed forces the opportunity to undertake badly needed reorganization and retraining of its personnel thereby making them effective against the insurgents. Under the pretext of the ceasefire, the CPP reorganized and redirected its strategies. Afraid that this might occur, the military insisted on a 30-day ceasefire as a longer period would give the CPP time to regroup. President Aquino declared that she was aware of this possibility, but was prepared to pursue negotiations to prevent any further hostilities (*Business Day*, 21 April 1986). During the ceasefire period, the NDF conducted an effective propaganda campaign in the media and as a result was able to communicate some of its objectives and appeal to the public. Indeed, access to the media was perceived to be important to "give greater. . . effectiveness to propaganda" (*Memoranda*, NDF July 1986). After the termination of the ceasefire, the military and other groups in the Philippines claimed that the CPP was winning the propaganda war against the AFP.

What concerns elements in the AFP is the recognition given to the Communists by the Aquino government through the ceasefire agreement and permission to participate in national politics. Under the Alliance for New Politics (ANP), leftist groups such as the *Partido ng Bayan* (PnB) People's Party, the Volunteers for Popular Democracy (VPD) and the cause-oriented umbrella organization *Bagong Alyansang Makabayan* (BAYAN) fielded candidates in the May 1987 national elections. According to the military, this amounted to awarding legitimate political status to the CPP thus enhancing its cause and encouraging the NDF to seek international support.

The 1988 visit by a Soviet diplomatic and trade delegations to the Philippines and discussions for facilities to dock their fishing vessels in Cebu are interpreted by the military as providing an avenue for the Soviet Union to give support to the CPP. But this appears unlikely as the CPP has avoided seeking assistance from other Communist countries, though it has recently been making overtures to obtain foreign assistance. For the Soviets, aiding the CPP would jeopardize its relationship with the Aquino government and indeed ASEAN, and could reverse its recent gains in international diplomacy. Moreover, the Aquino government is likely to be more favorable to the Soviets than a military-dominated regime. But the CPP would be likely to seek international material support should the military seize power since some observers allege that the CPP/NPA has reached a "plateau" and is incapable of fighting effectively against the AFP because of a lack of weaponry *(Asian Wall Street Journal*, 8 & 15 June 1988).

Presently, there is no consensus in the AFP on how to deal with the insurgency. This was highlighted in February 1988 when disagreement over this issue between the secretary of Defense, Ret. Gen. Rafael Ileto, and the AFP Chief of Staff Gen. Fidel Ramos, culminated in the resignation of the former and the latter acceding to the Defense portfolio. Yet this has not insured a unified approach to the insurgency.

Nevertheless, the predominant view in the AFP is for a civilian-military strategy with the military pursuing the armed campaign and, in conjunction with the civilian government agencies, addressing the socioeconomic problems. Civil-military operations (CMOs), which include education, propaganda and medical and dental care, are currently conducted solely by the military as the civilian agencies have failed to perform their functions. But with inadequate resources, the AFP cannot undertake both military and civilian functions successfully. Moreover, it is not the military's function to undertake socioeconomic reforms or establish political organizations. Rather, its mission is to maintain peace and order in the nation and protect it from internal and external enemies. It is not surprising, therefore, that people in the rural areas (where soldiers are often the only representatives of the government) are allegedly dissatisfied with the Aquino administration. Now that the soldiers are working closer with the people, the opportunity exists for them to exploit this dissatisfaction as they are aware that the CPP gains support by exploiting popular dissatisfaction with the government. The AFP desperately needs "to win the hearts and minds of the people" and it will use any method to achieve this objective. Despite the exposure and subsequent killings of AFP "deep penetration agents" in the CPP/NPA, the military in government is likely to continue using this method to create dissensions within the CPP and to spread anti-Communist feelings. The military perceives that it can now more easily change its image of "abuser" to that of "protector of the people" as a result of pay and allowance increases and financial assistance from business in some islands, such as Negros.

By winning and maintaining the people's trust the military claims it will rob the CPP of its support. In this "hearts and minds" campaign, the AFP is presently undertaking education and propaganda exercises. An example of this strategy is the stationing of seven-man Special Operations Teams (SOTs) in barangays infiltrated by the Communists.

18

According to the military, it realizes that the price of victory cannot be measured in terms of casualties and annihilation of enemy forces, but in the extent of people's support. Whoever wins that wholehearted support will win the war. To be sure the military desperately needs to be the winner, especially if it intends to govern.

Despite the emphasis on "the hearts and minds" campaign, there is a second method of fighting the insurgents favored by some officers, should a military regime assume office. This school of thought in the military argues that acquiescence can be gained through maximum repression. Indeed, the AFP is remembered for its violations of left-wing opponents during the martial law regime.

Some groups maintain that the military still continue to torture and kill Filipinos under the Aquino administration *(Task Force Detainees,* 1987). In an article, Prof. Al McCoy claims the "August [1987] coup exposed the importance of an ethos of violence in the RAM ideology." He cites conversations with RAM's chief political planner, Navy Capt. Rex Robles, who states it is necessary "to kill as many people as possible" to grab power (McCoy, 1988:22-23). Therefore, the armed campaign is likely to be increased. Yet it is doubtful whether the military will change its present strategy, and begin to initiate armed combat with the NPA. At present, NPA's policy is not to attack AFP units unless they are engaged in "anti-people and offensive military action." But whether this policy will be adhered to in the event of a military rule is uncertain. NDF representatives would not speculate on this situation.

B. The Muslim Insurgents

Elements in the military accuse the Aquino government of "reviving the Muslim Problem." They claim that Nur Misuari and the Moro National Liberation Front (MNLF) which he leads, were off the political agenda when Mrs. Aquino came to power. The AFP further claims that the MNLF does not represent all Muslims as they are divided into diverse ethno-linguistic groups. Even the Muslim rebels are divided into the MNLF, MNLF-Reformist Group (MNLF-RG), the Moro Islamic Liberation Front (MILF) and the Bangsa Minsupala Islamic Liberation Organization (BMILO) formerly the Islamic Bangsa Moro Liberation Organization (BMLO). Consequently, negotiations with Nur Misuari's MNLF, seen by the Aquino government as the key to the solution to the fourteen-year rebellion, were criticized by the MILF leader

Hashim Salamat (*The Economist*, 7 February 1987). Yet the agreement between the Aquino administration and the MNLF signed in January 1987 is apparently more credible to the Muslims than the 1976 Tripoli agreement signed between the Marcos administration and the MNLF, according to some representatives of the organization.

No single solution is, however, likely to resolve the grievances of the Muslims or put an end to the "problem." A full-scale military campaign will not be launched against the Muslims by a prospective military-dominated government as it would be met by opposition and international condemnation from Muslim nations. Additionally, fighting the NPA and the MNLF concurrently is likely to overextend the AFP. Accommodation with the Muslims can be attained through alleviating some of their grievances. Presently, the CMOs are conducted in these communities by soldiers who are members of the same ethnic group. According to the military, some form of autonomy is also necessary and will be addressed through a policy of federalism in the event of a military-dominated government. Autonomy could also result in the Muslims assisting the AFP to curb NPA activities. Cooperation between the military and Muslim rebels against the NPA has already occurred, although there are also examples of NPA-MNLF cooperation. For example, the highly respected Marines combined with members of the Islamic Bangsa Moro to exterminate NPA members in a zoning exercise in Davao City in January 1986 (*San Pedro Express*, 16 January 1986). But a military regime may also use a policy of divide and rule by exploiting inter- and intra-group rivalries in the Muslim community.

C. Business and Politicians

Land reform is an issue that demonstrates the political elites' inability to institute societal change in the Philippines. After three years in office the Aquino administration has not been able to resolve the land reform issue used by the Communists to gain adherents. New People's Army members often cite the inequitable land tenure system as a major reason for joining the organization. The AFP concedes that had President Aquino issued a land reform decree before Congress reconvened, it would have been policed by the armed forces. But the military claims that as President Aquino is a member of the landowning group it would not have been in her interest to pursue such a policy. Interestingly, the CPP has also accused President Aquino of being from a *"comprador-*

landlord class and thus unable to identify with the people" (*Mr. & Ms.*, Special Edition, 7-13 February 1987).

The "mangled version" of the Comprehensive Agrarian Reform Program (CARP) ratified by the Senate in March 1988 has been judged ineffective by the original sponsors who have now disassociated themselves from it (*Katipunan*, May 1988). The CARP has little support from landowners and peasants so it will not be effective in resolving the land reform issue. Landowners on the island of Negros are resistant to CARP and are prepared to oppose its imposition (*FEER*, 25 June 1987). They are once again forming private armies encouraged by, among others, US Ret. Gen. John Singlaub. The AFP is not objecting to this trend. For a military-dominated government, these militias could augment its forces and be used to "manage" opposition. Perhaps these militias could be used to oppose CARP or to support a military-dominated government in suppressing opposition?

Landowners and business groups on Negros have successfully courted the military by supplying divisions stationed there with badly-needed resources. In conjunction, they have established the BAC-UP Foundation (Bacolod Citizens for Unity and Peace) in Negros Occidental. Brigadier General Miguel Coronel, provincial commander of Negros, was instrumental in devising this organization to keep peace and order in the area. Supported by the Negros elite, buildings were provided which have been converted into garrison-type structures, manned by soldiers and, apparently unarmed civilians. Clerical staff and office materials have been provided to supplement military resources. In Negros, Gen. Rene G. Cardones, commander of Task Force Sugarland, needing more soldiers to patrol the villages, has supplemented his divisions by forming the Philippine Constabulary Forward Command (PCFC). Composed of former members of the Civilian Home Defense Forces (CHDF) and landowner-paid militia, the PCFC is augmenting the armed forces in Negros. From these activities it can be ascertained that planter power has been restored in Negros.

The success of these arrangements between the military, planters and businesses in Negros have encouraged military commanders from other islands to demand similar arrangements with landowners and businesses in their areas. In Mindanao, Lt. Col. Franco Calida, Philippine Constabulary commander of Davao City, denounced these groups for not supplying his detachment with badly needed resources. In retaliation he threatened to expose the names of Rotary Club members who contribute financial aid to the Communist rebels if they do not help his poorly equipped force. Business leaders are not in favor of taking the initiative to supply assistance to the military. They prefer the military to make the request. Thus, as the military division in an area realizes its dependence on businesses and landowners for realizes its dependence on businesses and landowners for resources, then the question arises: whose interests should the military protect in a crisis, those of the Aquino government or those of the local elite?

Filipino business leaders pledged their support for constitutional democracy after an address by President Aquino on 20 October 1987 at the Manila Hotel. Yet some businessmen have stated "we are in business for profit and because of this we are prepared to support the military in government if it can restore stability and economic growth." Authoritarian regimes in Asia and elsewhere in the Third World have demonstrated that they can provide an environment where economic development can occur. These regimes generally restrict trade union activity and impose stricter labor discipline while implementing policies favorable to investment. Landowners and businesses in the Philippines now have closer links with the armed forces through formal organizations such as the National Alliance for Democracy and Morality (ADAM) and the National Movement for Freedom and Democracy (NMFD) and through informal channels. The importance of these relationships can be ascertained from businesses' clandestine support of the RAM, which was perceived by business as an acceptable alternative to the Marcos regime. Therefore, landowners and businessmen could support a military-dominated government if it satisfies their interests.

A contributing factor in Marcos' long hold on power was the lack of a united opposition. This situation prevailed prior to the February 1986 elections, and until Salvador Laurel was persuaded to join forces with Mrs. Corazon Aquino to defeat President Marcos. But soon after the new administration assumed office, acrimony surfaced, political realignment began and disunity was once again evident. For example, the 1987 constitutional plebiscite was opposed by Aquino's first secretary of Defense, Juan Ponce Enrile, who had served in that capacity under former president Marcos and had recently organized the Grand Alliance for Democracy (GAD) party. Of relevance also is the fact that the military, which strongly identified with Enrile, voted overwhelmingly against the Constitution. Vice President Salvador Laurel, unable to temper his presidential ambitions with political pragmatism, was dropped from Aquino's cabinet and is pursuing his own political agenda to acquire the presidency. Factionalism in the government has a debilitating effect on the overall performance of the administration. Yet divisiveness continues to plague the cabinet with reports that members are being accused by others in the government of being "arrogant and uncooperative" *(Philippine Weekend Star*, 1-7 May 1988). Meanwhile, the president is also encountering criticism against her family's alleged involvement in corruption.

A multisectoral movement, *Unladbayan* or National Movement for Economic Reconstruction and Survival or Nation Movers, headed by businessman Enrique Zobel was formed in Manila in March 1988. Among its members are leaders of political parties such as GAD, United Nationalist Democratic Organization (UNIDO), the *Kilusang Bagong Lipunan* (KBL), and the Nacionalista Party (NP), and former Huk supremo Luis Taruc. This organization claims it has access to funding from overseas which could be utilized to retain the US military bases and make a government more efficient (*Katipunan*, May 1988 & *FEER*, 7 April 1988). Because the KBL (Marcos' political organization) is affiliated with Nation Movers, the organization expects to get financial assistance from Marcos and indeed the support of his loyalists. Concurrently, elements in the military still loyal to Marcos, also expect the same support from their former commander-in-chief. Allegedly, the GAD leaders claim they are prepared to participate in a military regime (*Pacific Defense Reporter*, March 1988). Members of Unladbayan undertook a speaking tour of the country in April 1988 to publicize its opposition to the government and to espouse its central thesis of federalism. In Mindanao, the secretary general of Unladbayan, Lito Banayo, a former postmaster general, emphasized the movement's commitment to a federalism which will benefit Mindanao (*Philippine Daily Globe*, 27 April 1988). Its representatives have already met with Moro National Liberation Front (MNLF) leaders. Commenting on the CARP, Unladbayan members claim that it will institute a policy that wil' be satisfactory to landlords (Katipunan, May 1988). From the views expressed by AFP officers and Unladbayan members, the two organizations appear to have much in common. Therefore, it is highly likely that they could cooperate in forming a regime. As Cardòso (1979:48) persuasively argues, "authoritarian regimes not based on a political party are sometimes too weak to cope with complex societies." Since the Unladbayan has incorporated leading members of the major political parties, the possibility of support for and limited organized opposition from these parties to a future military-dominated regime would appear to be minimal. Many politicians realize the difficulties the government is encountering in instituting changes. Furthermore, despite taking a more assertive role in government, President Aquino is still perceived by some Filipinos to be weak. Thus, there are questions over her ability to bring about stability. Some of these dissatisfied constituents might accept a more decisive leader. In fact, officers point out that strong leadership and commitment to the nation are imperative for development, as has been demonstrated by other successful Asian nations. In countries such as the Philippines where industrialization is still in its early phase, authoritarian regimes appear to provide an appropriate environment for economic development to occur. Historically, Philippine leaders such as the first president Emilio Aguinaldo, and Commonwealth president Manuel Quezon have demonstrated authoritarian tendencies (Gleeck, 1987:1-10). Filipino writer Leonardo Mercado has argued that if the Filipino family and society are authoritarian so must be the government if it is to be truly Filipino. A professor of political science at the University of the Philippines, Estrella Solidum, supports this argument and uses the example of other Asian countries as justification (Brillantes, 1987:10).

While agreeing with the military in its demands for strong leadership, some politicians claim that they do not support its desires for a military-dominated government. But officers claim that politicians are *balimbings* (which means politicians could be counted on to switch allegiance to gain political office). Historically there has been little ideological differences between political parties in the Philippines, though this could be changing. Therefore, it should not be difficult to gain support from some politicians, especially since there are retired officers in the present government, while others currently head government agencies. Examples of these are: Gen. Rodolfo A. Canieso at the National Intelligence Coordinating Service, Gen. Salvador Mison at the Bureau of Customs, Gen. Cesar Tapia and Rear Adm. Tagumpay Jardiniano at the Manila International Airport and the Bureau of Posts respectively. Lesser ranked officers are at Telecommunications, the Metro-Manila Transit and the Philippine Ports Authority. A number of former officers are now elected governors and mayors. Other politicians have worked closely with the military during the martial law regime, some have links through their immediate family and a number are courting the military in the event that they may have to work with it. Indeed these politicians are aware of the potential leadership problem to be faced by a military regime. As it is presently unable to find a leader from its ranks, the military is prepared to go into partnership with politicians and has proposed this idea to a number of them. Some politicians have acquiesced as they believe that by working in a military-dominated government it will be possible to "civilianize" it. But politicians are unlikely to have much power in the proposed regime since officers perceive themselves as being capable of adequately performing civilian tasks. In some Third World countries the military intervenes in politics because officers have a sense of superiority over civilian politicians, and regard themselves as more skilled and modernized than other sectors of society. In the Philippines superiority is not the issue, some officers, however, perceive themselves to be more modernized and skilled than some sectors of society.

In the Philippine military, the RAM members claim that politicians only make a mess of the country (*Ang Pahayagang Malaya*, 16 May 1985), thus displaying their contempt for politicians. During the martial law period officers were able to exert control over politicians because of the sweeping powers granted to them by presidential decrees especially in arresting and jailing political opponents of the regime. Now it appears that politicians are once again reasserting their control of the military. With the reconvening of Congress, the Commission on Appointments (CA) has been reestablished. This commission is comprised of senators and congressional representatives and determines all officers' promotions to full colonelcy. The majority of officers interviewed claim that "it [the CA] will only result in politicians again interfering in military affairs." Generally, officers attach great importance to their autonomy and believe civilians should be prohibited from trespassing on all military matters including appointments. Any action by the civilian government perceived as threatening the armed forces autonomy could generate opposition from the military and provide a cogent reason for unity within the AFP and motives for intervening in politics. Officers would prefer the abolition of the CA. But the commission is necessary to ensure civilian supremacy over the military as mandated by the Constitution, and will further assist in the building of civilian political control structures over the military. Such political control over the AFP would appear necessary for the survival of the Aquino government and indeed its civilian successors during periods of social and political change in the Philippines.

The RAM had proposed that Sen. Juan Ponce Enrile, a civilian politician, should head a military-dominated government. Perhaps it realized the problems encountered by military regimes in gaining the support of the people. Indeed, military governments have problems achieving and sustaining legitimacy. A narrow support base can be a great handicap as retaining control may come to rest entirely on the imposition of force. Legitimacy can best be acquired through mass support and participation. It is therefore accepted that politicians with popular credibility are essential in assisting a military-dominated government in its quest for legitimacy. But realizing that legitimacy may be elusive, a regime may initially seek acquiescence from the population. Popular acquiescence rather than legitimacy may be acceptable to a military-dominated regime (Van Doorn, 1975:87- 107).

Marcos tried to change the composition of local power structures in the Philippines by centralization, but in the process he created new power brokers. President Aquino forced some of those, such as Gov. Ali Dimaporo of Lanao del Sur, to resign. Yet this did not curb their influence. Rather many established elites in provincial areas are once again reasserting their authority. The military has been observing this re-emergence of provincial elite power and perceives this positively as it could be harnessed to assist a military-dominated government to maintain stability in the regions. The AFP could even delegate de facto control to these leaders. But it appears that a military-dominated regime may also give more power to provincial military commanders so that they can counter potential competition between rival warlords.

D. The Church

Relations between the Christian churches (i.e., the Roman Catholic and mainstream Protestant churches, herein referred to as the church,) and the AFP deteriorated as a result of the imposition of martial law and the violation of human rights by the armed forces. According to the military, the church had been infiltrated by Communists. The involvement of religious leaders in the insurgency problem was seen as clear evidence of this. Their relationship, however, improved as a result of the AFP's performance in the events at EDSA in February 1986. Jaime Cardinal Sin, head of the Roman Catholic Church, praised the new image of the AFP at a rally in Manila on 2 March 1986 (*US Foreign Relations Committee Report*, 1986). But relations deteriorated again after the attempted coups. Refocusing its objectives, ecclesiastic leaders are attempting to steer the church back to its more traditional spiritual role. But this may create further divisions in the church as conservative groups become further alienated from the radicals.

According to Youngblood (1984:215) the church is divided into "conservative, moderate and progressive" with 77 per cent of the hierarchy comprising the first two groups. Considering the cleavage in church-military relationship and indeed within the church itself, the response to a military-dominated government will be varied. The church hierarchy did not actively oppose the martial law regime until it was in its terminal stages. By then many Roman Catholic priests, nuns and lay religious workers had indicated their support for the Left, even to the extent of joining the NPA.

For the military, on the other hand, the church has lost much of its credibility because of its involvement in radical politics and it can only regain this by returning to its traditional role. Yet while taking measures to resume this posture, the church also needs to counter the influence of the charismatic religious movement presently spreading in the AFP and indeed in all sectors of the Philippine society. Some of these groups are perceived by the military as attending to the spiritual needs of their members in the proper manner. Some groups also donate funds for religious programs conducted by the AFP, and also provide a forum for officers to preach to the people. For example, Brig. Gen. Honesto Isleta, chief of the civil relations group at Camp Aguinaldo, is a preacher in the Full Gospel Businessmen's Fellowship (*FEER*, 12 March 1987). There are religious groups such as the Unification Church of Sun Myung Moon (called the Moonies), and the Asian Ecumenical Inter-Faith Council (alleged to be a front of the Moonies), which are avowedly anti-Communist and are prepared to actively support the military in its anti-Communist crusade. A military-dominated government espousing such a perspective will undoubtedly be supported by these groups.

If the influence of such groups become more pervasive in the military, the church would lose more support there. A number of Catholic chaplains in the AFP are concerned with this trend and have been trying to counter this influence. But many senior officers, including the former chief of staff and now Defense secretary, Ret. Gen. Fidel V. Ramos, a member of the Protestant United Church of Christ in the Philippines, subscribe to greater involvement of the church in the military. Therefore, the effects of probable church opposition to a military-dominated government is unpredictable, especially as the church will not be united in its approach. Some church members will resort to armed struggle. And without doubt the "culture of violence" elements in the military will adopt repressive methods against both those who are armed and others who are involved in working for social justice.

E. The Perceived Reactions from the Population

Finally, elements in the military claim that most Filipinos will adopt a "wait and see attitude" towards the imposition of a military-dominated government. Why? Because the most immediate concern of the estimated 65 per cent of Filipinos who live below the poverty line is to satisfy their basic needs of food and shelter. The Aquino government has done little to alleviate their situation and these people are becoming increasingly dissatisfied with the administration. Should this situation prevail, "the military's consciousness of themselves as a profession may lead them to see themselves as the servants of the state, rather than of the government in power" (Finer, 1975:22). When this occurs it would provide further justification for the military to try and displace the Aquino government. The AFP anticipates that poor socioeconomic conditions would facilitate popular manipulation by opposition groups and indeed the military, as was demonstrated during elections under President Marcos. Arguably so. Elements in the armed forces, however, claim that those who are prepared to be exploited by opposition groups will be repressed. Military regimes use repression to achieve submission. For a prospective regime, the plan will be similar to that envisaged for the "God Save the Queen" coup attempt in November 1986 when armored vehicles were to patrol the streets to prevent any demonstrations of "people power" (*Business Day*, 7 November 1986). Filipinos remember the military's record for repressing opposition during the martial law regime. Therefore, whether they will want to risk invoking his wrath again, or whether they will "wait and see," can only be determined if a military-dominated regime governs.

5

INTERNATIONAL RESPONSE

Experience has demonstrated that the immediate reaction of many Western democratic countries to a military-dominated government is criticism. Some nations suspend while others break diplomatic relations. If, however, stability can be quickly restored then popular acquiescence can be interpreted as legitimacy and international recognition is automatic. And when major international powers recognize a regime, other less influential nations tend to follow.

A. US Recognition

For a prospective military-dominated government in the Philippines, US recognition is crucial. A regime cannot survive without American support. Indeed, some will argue, that plans to install a military-dominated regime in the Philippines cannot occur without the tacit approval of the administration in Washington. The United States plays a major role in the Philippine economy through investment and aid. Early in 1988, the Reagan administration planned to implement an international aid program for the Philippines. The program has been compared to the 1947 Marshall plan which contributed to the reconstruction of Western Europe after the Second World War, and is subsequently referred to as the "mini-Marshall plan." Proposed by Cong. Stephen Solarz and Sen. Allan Cranston of the United States, it aims to enlist financial assistance from America's European allies, and countries in the Asian region such as Australia, Japan and South Korea. Other ASEAN governments have also pledged to contribute to the scheme which intends to supply US $1 billion a year to the Philippines over a five-year period. Before the proposal is finalized, an American delegation will visit the country. How dependent the approval of the scheme is on the retention of the US military bases in the Philippines beyond the expiry of the current treaty in 1991 has not yet been determined. But it is doubtful whether the US will still be interested in pursuing the program if the bases were to be transferred from the Philippines, since these are its major interest in the country.

Any US administration expects Philippine governments to allow the military bases to remain. Significantly the new Philippine Constitution endorsed in 1987 is ambiguous about the status of the American bases at Clark Field and Subic Bay. On 5 April 1988 the five-yearly review of the military bases agreement began in Manila. Signed in 1947, the agreement commits the Philippines to host six US military installations until 1991. Demands for terms more favorable to the Philippines by its chief negotiator, Secretary of Foreign Affairs Raul Manglapus, and anti-US demonstrations by the Campaign for a Sovereign Philippines, a left-center coalition of base opponents, made it difficult to predict the results of these discussions. In addition, President Aquino has not committed herself to the retention or dismantling of the bases after 1991. Despite the difficult negotiations the agreement was finally signed. But a bill to ban nuclear weapons and nuclear-powered ships from the Philippines approved by the Philippine Senate in June 1988 could compound problems between the Bush administration and the Aquino government. Should the bill hamper the US military activities in the region, then the administration in Washington will have to decide whether it can abide by the legislation or contemplate supporting a regime that would not make such demands on the US government.

Meanwhile, the AFP is in favor of retaining the bases, although it would like an increase in "rental" (the US calls it "aid") and claims that this is the preference of the majority of Filipinos. The Unladbayan members' declared policy on the bases is also for their retention. For the armed forces, retention of the bases would mean the continued injection of US $1.38 million a day into the Philippine economy which makes the US the country's second largest employer. Also assured would be the US supply of logistics and training to the AFP. Moreover, the US makes up the deficit in Philippine defense spending and has assisted in the modernization of the AFP. If the bases are removed then military aid and credit could be severely curtailed. The military needs this assistance as it is in no position to achieve self-reliance. Neither is it capable of managing the external defense of the nation. A US State Department report states that the AFP would require US $1.5 billion to make it effective against the NPA. Considering that the AFP is determined to defeat the Communists it will desperately need that assistance. During the Reagan administration the aid was slow in reaching the AFP. Perhaps this was because the Reagan administration had been skeptical about President Aquino's anti-Communist strategy and because it did not support the ceasefire agreement. Like the Marcos regime, a military-dominated government is prepared to demonstrate to an administration in Washington that it can be the bulwark against Communism in the Philippines and the defender of American interests. Apart from the overt aid the US gives to the AFP, assistance is also provided in areas such as access to US intelligence, which is necessary in the fight against the insurgents. Additionally, visits to the US are provided for senior AFP officers to familiarize them with current US attitude on the Philippine situation.

Evidence of possible US toleration for a military-dominated government in the Philippines was provided by retired and active duty officers and from the activities of US military personnel in the Philippines. For example, in 1987, a senior retired US military officer visited the Philippines and held discussions with a select number of senior AFP officers on active duty. In these discussions he is alleged to have said "the US administration is disappointed with the Aquino government." A few months later Maj. Victor Rafael, a US Defense Intelligence Agency officer in the Philippines, was accused by members of the Aquino administration of interfering in Philippine internal politics. Rafael apparently tried to persuade government troops not to fire on rebel soldiers involved in the 28 August 1987 coup (Bello, 1987:80) which came dangerously close to toppling the Aquino government. Gregorio Honasan, who led this coup, is the leader of RAM. It has been alleged that the RAM was courted, and some of its activities funded, by the United States. But only the inner circle of the organization, which functions on three levels, was involved in this agreement as the other groups objected to outside interference. The US apparently only supported the movement because of its stated desire of restoring professionalism to the military. President Marcos, on the other hand, had repeatedly refused to institute reforms to professionalize the AFP, despite US requests. In keeping with its foreign policy practices, the US always maintains other options in Third World societies in case the existing government no longer satisfies US foreign policy objectives. In the Philippines, the RAM was that option during the latter stages of the Marcos regime. Although it lost some of its credibility and support in the AFP, because of its serious miscalculations during the 28 August 1987 coup, the RAM, or at least similar reform groups in the armed forces still remain an option for the US.

Clearly the US did not oppose the imposition of martial law in the Philippines, although it had an indication of President Marcos' intentions (Bonner, 1987:4 & 96). From that period President Marcos relied on the armed forces to retain power. In fact, US investments in the Philippines and aid to the regime increased. In addition, the US ignored requests from prominent Filipinos and international groups to pressure Marcos to lift martial law. Instead, during a state visit to the Philippines in July 1981, then Vice Pres. George Bush of the United States praised Marcos for his adherence to democracy. In a similar show of support for the regime in 1983, former US secretary of state, George Schultz, reiterated this sentiment (McDougald, 1987:240 & 174). Therefore, it can be surmised that the US is likely to support a military-dominated regime in the Philippines.

Despite some publicly critical comments, US recognition of military regimes in the Third World is usually granted, especially when a regime is considered America's "bastard son." The US needs to have its interests protected in the Philippines. Therefore, according to former US ambassador to the Philippines, William Sullivan, "a coup might presumably be supported on the grounds that the military identifies with US strategic interests, and would assure American access to the military bases" *(Foreign Policy*, 1983/84:153). If this can be assured, recognition of a military-dominated government in the Philippines could be guaranteed.

B. ASEAN and Other Asian Nations

Professor Estrella Solidum has argued that other Asian states have achieved development under authoritarian leadership. As an Asian nation, the Philippines would also benefit from authoritarian leadership (Brillantes, 1987:10).

During the 14 years under martial rule, the Philippines remained a member of the Association of South East Asian Nations (ASEAN). Yet the regime was never criticized by the leaders of these countries. In fact, support for former president Marcos from other ASEAN leaders was clearly demonstrated during a head of states meeting held in Manila in 1974, two years after martial law was declared. According to the military, it maintained peace and order and ensured that the meeting was successful for President Marcos and the Philippines. It was again able to demonstrate its ability to provide stability during the third ASEAN summit held in Manila in December 1987, despite fears of disruptions from leftist and rightist elements.

On this and previous occasions, President Aquino's policy on the Communists has been questioned by other ASEAN leaders. Singapore's Prime Minister Lee Kuan Yew and Indonesia's President Suharto have openly declared their preference for tougher measures to be taken against the Communists. Indeed, President Suharto expressed uneasiness over President Aquino's reconciliation policy with the Communists during her visit to Indonesia in August 1986. These leaders are aware that their stance is in line with that of the AFP.

Some ASEAN leaders have also expressed their preference for the US military bases to remain in the Philippines or at least in the region, especially in view of such incidents as the China-Vietnam Spratly Islands clash on 14 March 1988. Although not critical of Mrs. Aquino for "keeping her options open," ASEAN leaders would have preferred some commitment either way. On the other hand, the military's preference for the retention of the bases is clear. For ASEAN and other pro-Western Asian countries, the US military bases represent regional stability and serve as a counterbalance to the Soviet naval installation at Cam Ranh Bay in Vietnam, and are seen as necessary for maintaining the momentum of economic development. To support these claims, the Asia-Pacific Chamber of Commerce passed a resolution in 1987 acknowledging the importance of the US military bases for the security and stability of the region and the importance of such conditions for continued investment. Additionally, other Asian nations are concerned that if the US reduces its military forces in the region then Japanese forces will necessarily increase; and there is suspicion over Japanese militarism. Without a clear commitment from the Aquino government on the US military installations, regional uncertainty is likely to prevail, threatening economic growth. Should regional instability threaten economic growth as a result of the Aquino government's vacillation over the US military bases, then ASEAN leaders could possibly refrain from criticizing the AFP if it seeks to establish a military-dominated regime which is in favor of retaining the bases. Interestingly, during the 28 August 1987 coup attempt, ASEAN leaders, especially Indonesia and Thailand were slow in offering support to the Aquino administration (*FEER*, 10 September 1987).

Among the Asian states Japan needs special mention. It is the second largest foreign investor in the Philippines after the US, and has not increased its investments there significantly since Mrs. Aquino became president, in spite of expressed intentions to do so. President Aquino visited Tokyo in November 1987 to encourage closer relations between the two nations and to demonstrate that stability had returned to the society. But the plans for a coup while she was there robbed her of this opportunity. In 1988 a Japanese business delegation undertook a fact-finding mission to determine the prospects for increasing investments in the Philippines. To date Japan has not announced any new investment plans for the Philippines. A retired officer who advised the previous government on security matters speculated that increased Japanese investment and aid to the Aquino administration is linked with the US military installations, as Japan's preference is for them to remain in the Philippines. Stability would seem to be a prerequisite for investment, and perhaps the Aquino government has not demonstrated this to Japanese investors. Yet economic recovery is President Aquino's major hope of eliminating popular support for the Communist and other opposition groups. Whether a military-dominated regime can achieve this objective and ensure that economic development takes place, can only be determined if it governs. But it is difficult to perceive how such a regime could be more successful than the Aquino administration in gaining the confidence of foreign investors and achieving economic development.

6

FUTURE PROSPECTS

During its early years the armed forces were predominantly occupied with its internal development, which was largely undertaken by the United States. A semblance of autonomy from the United States was evident in the military after the country achieved independence in 1946. But the former colonial power exerted control over the AFP as a result of the inability of the Philippines to equip and maintain an independent armed force. Oriented towards external defense, the armed forces soon had to direct its attention to internal conflict when the Hukbalahap movement threatened the nation. Curtailed mostly because of US direction and assistance in the sociopolitical, economic and military campaign, the Huks surceased their activities and the AFP attained a significant role in government policy-making and national development. Comfortable with gaining this status, with US acquiescence, the military became an important element of the government as many officers performed political functions while on active duty. Reluctantly they returned to managing the external and internal security of the nation when this period was abruptly terminated with the death of the civilian president Ramon Magsaysay. But many officers were not willing to accept that the military should not continue to play a role in government policy-making and consistently tried to destabilize the administrations which curtailed its budget, size and role in government between 1957 and 1965.

The importance of the military as an ally in maintaining political power was realized by President Marcos who quickly provided it with a prominent role in society. With martial law this role increased significantly and most of the officer corps was again in agreement that the military should contribute to the development of the society and participate in government policy-making. President Marcos acquiesced. From then onwards the AFP's involvement in politics shifted from influence to participation (Hernandez, 1985a). In the process, however, "a misunderstanding of the constitutional principle of civilian supremacy over the military developed," resulting in the armed forces abandoning the president, according to Lt. Col. Benjamin Ambalong (1988).

Entrenched in national development and government policy-making by 1986, it was certainly ambitious to expect officers socialized into these functions to be relegated to relative obscurity, especially when the role of the AFP in contributing to the demise of the Marcos regime, and the accession of Aquino to the presidency is taken into consideration. Since the AFP had played such an important role in determining national politics, it could undoubtedly do so again. Moreover, commanders of the AFP appointed in the next decade will be from the group that was socialized into a military that was accustomed to participating in the formulation of government policy. Aware of this, President Aquino has been trying to redirect officers to performing the military's function, which, she argued in her speech to the PMA graduating class in March 1988, is "Fighting the enemies. Policy making," she continued, "is the business of civilians." And "so long as this distinction is kept in mind, there will be no misunderstanding."

The idea of destabilizing the Aquino administration through attempted coups was not conceived because elements in the AFP wanted to establish a military junta, since the AFP had proposed that a civilian would head any future regime. Quite simply sections of the AFP wanted to play a larger role in society, as the military had been accustomed to for a considerable period of its existence, but not necessarily to establish a government dominated by officers. Additionally, Professor Nemenzo (1986:23) rightly asserts, "More likely the purpose was not even to depose Cory but just to pressure her to grant them a share of power commensurate to the role they played in the February [1986] Revolution;" a point of view supported by Lande and Hooley (1986:1095). On the other hand, the PMA Alumni Association has argued that the military was seeking "good government," while the Aquino administration was busy trying to curtail the armed forces' "alleged political ambitions" (*The POOP*, January-February 1987).

In accordance with the 1987 Constitution active duty officers are prohibited from participating in government. The Aquino administration has, however, tried to satisfy this desire and to avert those elements wanting to seize power by appointing retired officers to government positions. Among the most significant appointees are the retired generals presently in the Department of Foreign Affairs, Bureau of Customs, Department of National Defense, Commission on Immigration and Deportation, National Telecommunications Commission, and Department of Transportation and Communications. Significant among these is the elevation to secretary of Defense of Ret. Gen. Fidel Ramos who does not have widespread support in the AFP, especially in the army.

Whether such appointments will avert future coup attempts, or satisfy those demanding that the military play a more prominent role in government, will depend on how significant elements in the officer corps consider to be the influence the AFP has on the Aquino government. But the prospects for the military to be relegated to an insignificant position will not be achievable in the near future if the Muslim and Communist insurgency movements continue to try to destabilize the government. Moreover, if the Aquino or any future administrations are perceived to be incapable of curbing the insurgents, or in fact allow them to become influential in government, and the AFP perceive that the insurgents present a serious threat to the nation, then the possibility for the military returning to partnership in government or establishing a military-dominated regime is quite likely. Once its interests are satisfied, US support, vital for the existence of any Philippine government, will be provided in such an event, judging from previous experiences here and in other developing nations.

In this context, the continued stationing of the US military installations in the Philippines looms large. The present treaty expires in 1991, and negotiations will start in the preceding year. In the meantime, the US, wanting the bases to remain in the Philippines, is trying to influence various groups to support the retention of the bases. Of all the groups in the society, the AFP needs the least persuasion. Dependent on the US for training and equipment, among other things, the majority of the officer corps favors the retention of the installations since it means continued US aid. This was clearly evident during the prolonged bases negotiations in Manila in 1988 when a letter expressing support for the retention of the bases was published in the *Manila Bulletin* on 27 June, signed by a group of disgruntled officers. If the decision in 1991 is for the bases to be dismantled because of pressure on the Philippine government by nationalist group, rather than by mutual agreement between the US and the Philippines, then the Philippine government will have to give careful consideration of the reaction from the AFP, especially as the Communist insurgency is not expected to have subsided by then despite claims by the AFP that the insurgency will be curbed by 1991. Moreover, if the US perceives it necessary for the military installations to remain in the Philippines, then its actions will also warrant careful scrutiny. Some American risk analysts already speculate on the possibility of an attempted coup should relations between the two countries become critical in the near future (*South*, February 1989:45). The United States administrations are not averse to acting against Third World governments, by supporting pro-US political factions and the military to displace these governments when the US national interest is perceived to be at risk. Chile provides a classic example.

Presidential elections are scheduled for 1992. President Aquino claimed that she will not contest these elections, but that is yet to be determined. Should Aquino decide not to run for re-election, it is possible that she could support the Defense secretary, Ret. Gen. Fidel Ramos, or indeed the Speaker of the House, Cong. Ramon Mitra. But it is widely known that the president feels indebted to Ramos since he saved her government from a number of coup attempts. The retired general claimed that he has not made a decision on whether he will contest the presidential elections. Realizing the importance of military support, and universally popular in the AFP, Ramos, in the meantime, will ensure that he continues to play an important role in the selection of the next AFP Chief of Staff and all the service chiefs. The tour of duty of the present chief of staff, General de Villa, has already been extended, causing some friction in the military. It seems likely that Ramos could avoid a repetition of this situation in order to prevent increasing the friction between the armed forces and government. Given that those officers to be promoted have been nurtured by retired General Ramos, support from the military may be achieved in the event that he decides to contest the presidential elections. Considering that Ramos does not have a political party as a base, the military is important to him for this purpose, at least for the short term. But with Aquino's support he is likely to acquire the backing of the *Laban ng Demokratikong Pilipino*

(LDP) party and immediately have a political base (*FEER*, 9 March 1989).

The possibility of Ramos using the AFP as his political base depends on the state of the insurgency and the developments in the society as retired officers, despite shedding their uniforms, retain their allegiance to the armed forces. With his control over the AFP analogous to Ramon Magsaysay's in that position, the likelihood of Ramos emulating him are obvious. But given his avowed commitment to democracy, Ramos is more likely to use the AFP to suppress the NPA and accept the credit, and like Magsaysay, use the military as a vehicle to the presidency. It is necessary, however, to note that despite his public statements, Magsaysay was not opposed to staging a coup if it was the only method of achieving power. Considering Ramos' preference for the Philippines to maintain close links with the US, Washington may support his bid for the presidency. Depending on the proclivity of the majority of the AFP officer corps, they may expect Ramos, if elected, to accommodate their desires to play a more significant role in politics, and Ramos may acquiesce with implicit agreement from the US.

What the future Philippine governments need to recognize is that elements in the officer corps of the AFP perceive themselves capable of playing a more important role in government and will continue to try and achieve it. The AFP officers' perception on governing developed by virtue of their experience and education. Many argue, their education is equivalent to that of the technocrats. And indeed many officers are educated in Western military schools, mostly in the US, which encourage them to play a more prominent role in the economic and sociopolitical development of their societies.

Considering the perception of some of the officers, it is difficult to expect them to concentrate solely on the military mission of defending the nation. According to a senior officer, "The AFP can never go back to the barracks." Rather, officers can still be "engaged in certain civilian jobs that would be dangerous to civilians, especially in insurgency-wracked areas" (*The POOP*, January-February 1987). Arguments that officers cannot cope with civilian politics because it requires bargaining, compromise and skill in communication (Lissak, 1975:49) are no longer relevant in contemporary officership. Most officers are highly educated and schooled in the art of government. President Aquino, however, stated in her speech at the PMA in March 1988 that there must be a clear distinction between military and civilian functions. Accordingly, she avers, "I want a clear-cut division of labor; civilian department to civilian reconstruction, the military arm to military action."

Despite such pronouncements, it is unlikely that Philippine governments will simply be able to return the AFP to performing a purely military function in the immediate future. Once a military is accustomed to playing a significant role in politics, it is extremely difficult to break the habit. President Aquino had to accept to meet representatives of the RAM in January 1987 to listen to their grievances against the government, and later agreed to relieve members of the administration perceived by the AFP to be sympathetic to the Left. Furthermore, in a letter to the chief of staff, the RAM reminded the administration that the military is still part of the government (*FEER*, 12 February 1987). Elements of the AFP cite examples of other Third World nations such as South Korea, Indonesia and Thailand, where the armed forces have been successful in government or as participants. In fact, a US State Department official declared that "the Philippine army has become a Southeast Asian Army in the mode of Thailand and Indonesia. It feels it knows better than the civilians how to run the country" (*FEER*, 24 September 1987). Therefore it appears more realistic for political leaders to accept the politicization of the military and to encourage the AFP hierarchy to slowly socialize officer cadets to discontinue expectations to be involved in national policy-making. To curtail their expectations, however, Professor Nemenzo (1986:25) provides a more terse remedy, stating that "now that our soldiers have been politicized, we might as well politicize them properly. They should be made aware of the disastrous consequences of military rule in other countries; and how military intervention, far from solving any problem, compounds and makes it worse." But there are also examples of armed forces such as South Korea, Indonesia and Thailand in Asia, and elsewhere, which have contributed to the development of their country. Even military regimes which have been criticized, such as Chile and Brazil, have achieved economic growth and aspired to attain "social equity" in the society (Horowitz, 1981:40). Interestingly, the group in the AFP that desires to participate in governing only uses the military regimes that have been successful in developing their societies such as South Korea.

7

CONCLUSION

The AFP had some involvement in governing the Philippines during the term of President Magsaysay, but became a full partner in government with President Marcos after the declaration of martial law. From these experiences, some officers of the AFP have acquired skills to govern and the perception that the military can and will govern the Philippines. Further justification for determining the AFP's right to govern is based on the premise that the military's role was central to Marcos abandoning the presidency to Mrs. Aquino.

Yet whether the AFP can or will govern is dependent upon a number of factors. Foremost among these must be the ability of the group that perceives itself capable of governing to persuade or coerce a large section of the military, especially the army, to seize power. Given the present situation where factionalism keeps the organization divided, achieving unity may seem unlikely. But supposing unity is achieved and the military seizes power, the possibility will still exist for counter-coups. Then opposition from groups within the society will make governing difficult. Inter-factional tension in the armed forces may result in the country experiencing a series of coups before stability is restored, if it is restored at all.

If the Aquino administration continues to be perceived by the AFP and the majority of Filipinos as incapable of instituting change or curbing the Communist threat, then dissatisfaction with it will increase. Generally a perceived failure of the democratic system to resolve the problems of the Philippines could result in a restoration of authoritarianism. The AFP is already trying to improve its image with the people while elements professing the rights to govern have contingency plans and will capitalize on any crisis in the society to achieve government.

Indeed, it is under conditions of political and social crisis that the opportunity exists for the military to seize power because, under these circumstances, the capacity of the civilian government to withstand pressure from the military is less than normal conditions. Certain elements in the AFP have been strengthening their links with organizations opposed to the Aquino government, and have courted politicians sympathetic to their cause. Realizing the importance of the role of the US in determining the future of any government in the Philippines, the military has made its policy on the US military installations in the islands known to Washington. Some officers believe that the AFP demonstrated its ability to guarantee stability in the country during the ASEAN leaders meeting in Manila in 1987, and in the process the military was signalling to those countries its capabilities. These leaders' views on the hardline approach to Communism and on the US military installations are in alignment with that of the AFP's.

But whether the group in the AFP professing its ability and right to govern can institute changes when in government is debatable. Third World military regimes have not generally made drastic changes in socioeconomic patterns of these societies while politically their authoritarian style of governing has created more dissension than consensus. The groups with which the military is currently aligning itself in the Philippines are unlikely to implement major socioeconomic changes should they participate in government. Therefore, while the AFP is criticizing the Aquino government for its inability to address issues that augment the NPA ranks, it is difficult to see how a military-dominated government will be different. Plans for the composition of a proposed military-dominated government cannot be applauded by the majority of Filipinos. The benefits will be for a privileged group of civilians and officers. What is likely to emerge in the Philippines, in the event that a military-dominated regime govern, is accommodation between the military and certain elite groups. New power brokers will emerge as will cronyism and new dynasties. The majority of Filipinos will experience few socioeconomic benefits. Popular acquiescence to the regime could be demanded through repression. But the most important change in society will be the assertion by the AFP of its right to determine the composition and tenure of future governments in the Philippines.

Appendix 1

PHILIPPINES: SCHEMATIC CHART OF COMMAND RELATIONSHIPS OF DEFENSE AND POLICE AGENCIES

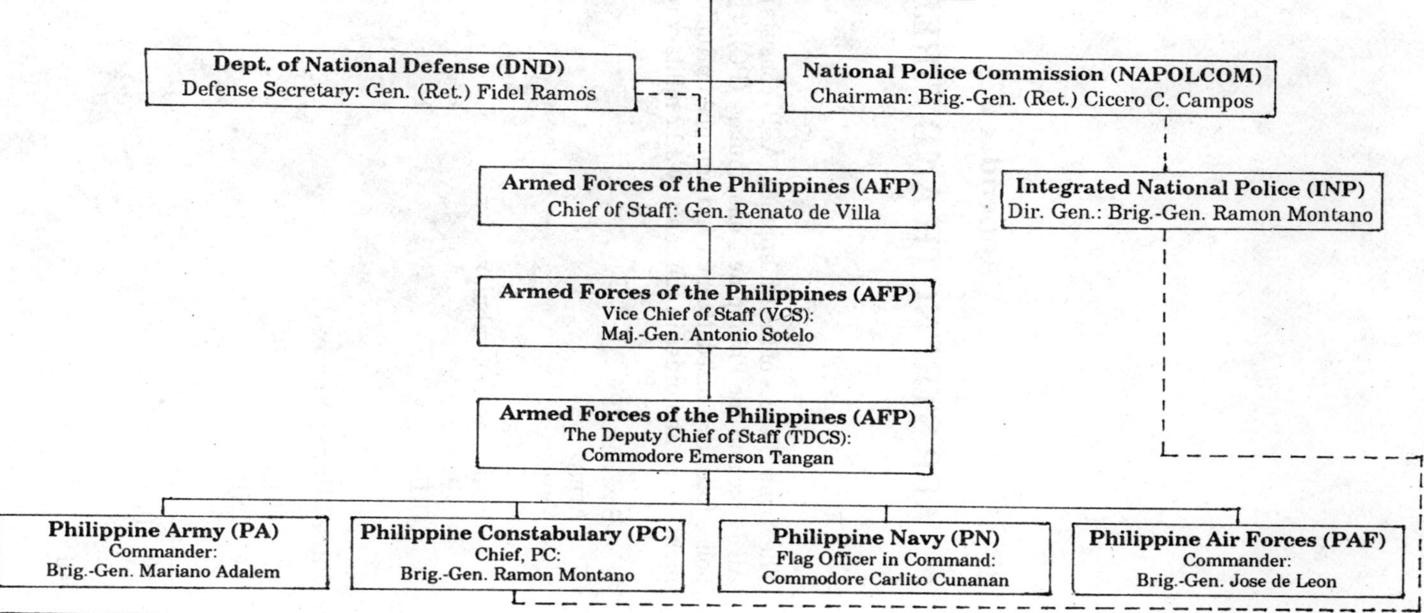

NOTE: Organizational set-up as of July 1988

Appendix 2

AFP STRENGTH AND FIREPOWER[*]

The Armed Forces of the Philippines (AFP) consists of the Army, Navy, Air Force and the Philippine Constabulary (PC). The PC is a national police force organized, trained and equipped primarily for the enforcement of law and order in the country's 12 military regions.

Size of AFP	257,000
Army	62,000
Navy	28,000
Air Force	16,000
Philippine Constabulary	54,000
INP	52,000
CHDF	45,000

Paramilitary Forces

CHDF	45,000
INP	52,000

---

[*]Data as of July 1988

Officers vs. Rank and File

Officers	16,000
Rank and File	196,000
Rank and File per Officer	12.2

Note: For every soldier in actual combat, seven more are in administrative duties.

Reserve Forces

Total	124,000
Army	96,000
Navy	12,000
Air Force	16,000

Firepower

Armored Vehicles	410
Tracked	286
Wheeled	130

Aircraft

Fixed Wing (F5, Tora-Tora)	143
Rotary (Sikorsky and Hueys)	74

AFP ORGANIZATION

Army

5 Infantry Divisions
First Scout Ranger Regiment
82 Infantry Battalions

Philippine Constabulary

13	Regional Commands
225	Provincial Companies

Navy

7	Frigates
10	Corvettes
13	Patrol Crafts
6	Task Force (normally composed of one flag ship, two patrol ships, one landing ship to move troops and hardware and smaller patrol craft).

Air Force

51	Combat Aircraft
16	Armed Helicopters
1	Squadron with 12 F-8H
1	Squadron with 10 F-5A
2	Infantry Battalions

DEFENSE SPENDING

	Percentage of Total Government Spending	Percentage of Gross National Product
1971-1975	18.88	1.92
1976-1980	14.42	2.32
1981-1985	9.70	1.58

References

Ambalong, Benjamin. 1988. "Military Revolt: An Analysis." Unpublished paper. National Defense College of the Philippines.

Ang Pahayagang Malaya, 16 May 1985.

Asian Wall Street Journal, 8 and 15 June 1988.

Bello, Walden, 1987. *Creating the Third Force: US Sponsored Low Intensity Conflict in the Philippines.* San Francisco: Institute for Food and Development Policy.

Bonner, Raymond, 1987. *Waltzing with a Dictator: The Marcoses and the Making of American Policy.* New York: Times Books.

Brillantes, Alex B., Jr., 1987. *Dictatorship and Martial Law: Philippine Authoritarianism in 1972.* Quezon City: Great Books.

Business Day, 21 April and 7 November 1986.

Cardoso, Fernando H., 1979. "On the Characteristics of Authoritarian Regimes in Latin America," in E. Collier ed. *The New Authoritarianism in Latin America.* Princeton: Princeton University Press.

Chai-Anan, S. 1982. *The Thai Young Turks.* Singapore: Institute of South East Asian Studies.

Constantino, R. and L. R., 1984. *The Philippines: The Continuing Past.* Quezon City: Foundation for Nationalist Studies.

CPP Memoranda from the Executive Committee, 23 December 1985, in "What the CPP/NPA Say About Elections: 'Boycott and Launch Military Operations,'" *Mr. & Ms.* Special Edition, 7-13 February 1987.

Crisol, Jose M. and Uldarico S. Baclagon, 1983. *Valor: World War II Saga of Ferdinand E. Marcos.* Quezon City: Development Academy of the Philippines.

de Dios, A., 1988. "Intervention and Militarism," in A. Javate-de Dios et al. (eds.). *Dictatorship and Revolution: Roots of People's Power.* Metro Manila: Conspectus.

Doorn, Jaques van, 1975. *The Soldier and Social Change.* Beverly Hills: Sage Publications.

The Economist, 7 February 1987.

Far Eastern Economic Review (FEER), 12 February, 12 and 26 March, 25 June, 24 September 1987; and 9 March 1989.

The Financial Post, 27 November 1987.

Finer, Samuel, 1975. *The Man on Horseback: The Role of the Military in Politics.* Penguin Books. Middlesex: Penguin Books.

Garcia, Eduardo M., 1988. "Can a Politicized Military Be Avoided?" Unpublished paper.

Gleeck, Lewis E., 1987. *President Marcos and the Philippine Political Culture.* Manila: Loyal Printing.

Goldberg, Sherwood D., 1976. "The Bases of Civilian Control of the Military in the Philippines," in Claude E. Welch, ed., *Civilian Control of the Military: Theory and Cases from Developing Countries.* Albany: State University of New York.

Hernandez, Carolina G., 1985. "The Philippine Military and Civilian Rule Under Marcos and Beyond," *Third World Quarterly,* 7(4).

__________, 1985. "The Philippines," in Z. H. Ahmad and H. Crouch (eds.), *Military-Civilian Relations in South-East Asia.* London: Oxford University Press.

Katipunan, May 1988 and FEER, 7 April 1988.

Lande, C. H. and Hooley, R. 1986. "Aquino Takes Charge," *Foreign Affairs.* Summer.

Lissak, M. 1975. "Center and Periphery in Developing Countries and Prototypes of Military Elites," in K. Fidel (ed.), *Militarism in Developing Countries.* New Jersey: Transaction Books.

Luttak, E., 1968. *Coup D'Etat: A Practical Handbook.* London: The Penguin Press.

Manila Bulletin, 27 June 1988.

McCoy, A. W., 1987. "After the Yellow Revolution: Filipino Elite Factions and the Struggle for Power," in P. Krinks (ed.), *The Philippines Under Aquino.* Canberra: The Australian Development Studies Network.

__________, 1988. "RAM Boys: The Politicization of the Philippine Armed Forces." Unpublished paper presented at the Asian Studies Association of Australia Conference at the Australian National University, Canberra, Australia. February 1988.

McDougald, Charles C., 1987. *The Marcos File: Was He a Philippine Hero or a Corrupt Tyrant?* San Francisco: San Francisco Publishers.

Memoranda Executive Committee of the National Democratic Front on the Ceasefire Negotiations, July 1986.

Miranda, Felipe B. and Ruben F. Ciron, 1987. "Development and the Military in the Philippines in a time of Continuing Crisis." Quezon City. *Social Weather Stations Occasional Paper.*

Muego, B. N., 1987. "Fraternal Organizations and Factionalism within the Armed Forces of the Philippines," in *Asian Survey* 14(3) FALL.

Nemenzo, F., 1986. "A Nation in Ferment: Analysis of the February Revolution," in M. Rajaretnam (ed.), *The Aquino Alternative.* Singapore: Institute of Southeast Asian Studies.

__________, 1987. "A Season of Coups: Reflections on the Military in Politics," *Kasarinlan,* Philippine Quarterly of Third World Studies. Third World Studies Center, University of the Philippines.

__________, 1988. "From Autocracy to Elite Democracy," in A. Javate-de Dios et al. (eds.), *Dictatorship and Revolution: Roots of People's Power.* Metro Manila: Conspectus.

Nordlinger, Eric A., 1977. *Soldiers in Politics: Military Coups and Government.* Englewood Cliffs: Prentice Hall.

Pacific Defense Reporter, March 1988.

Philippine Daily Globe, 12, 26 and 27 April 1988.

Philippine Military Academy Alumni Association Inc., 1987. *The POOP.* January-February.

Philippine Weekend Star, 1-7 May 1988.

San Pedro Express, 16 January 1986.

South, February 1989.

Statement by Richard Armitage in *US Foreign Relations Committee Report 1986.*

Sullivan, William H., 1983/84. "Living without Marcos," *Foreign Policy,* 53.

Task Force Detainees 1987. *Statistical Report on Human Rights Violations for the First Quarters and Philippines Human Rights Update,* Vol. 2, No. 5.

Veritas, 19-25 March 1987.

Youngblood, Robert L., 1984. "Church and State in the New Republic of the Philippines," *Journal of Contemporary Southeast Asia,* 6(3).

OTHER RELATED NEW DAY PUBLICATIONS

The American Governors-General and High Commissioners in the Philippines **by Lewis E. Gleeck, Jr.**

At the Edge of Southeast Asian History **by James Warren**

Dissolving the Colonial Bond **by Lewis E. Gleeck, Jr.**

The February Revolution and Other Reflections **by Miguel A. Bernad, S.J.**

The Huk Rebellion **by Benedict J. Kerkvliet**

Philippine Revolution 1986 **by Douglas J. Elwood**

The United States and the Philippines **by Stephen R. Shalom**